SELECTED POEMS

by

SIEGFRIED SASSOON

faber and faber

First published in 1968
by Faber and Faber Limited
3 Queen Square London WC1N 3AU
Reprinted 1970, 1972, 1976, 1979, 1982, 1985 and 1988

Printed in Great Britain by
Richard Clay Ltd, Bungay, Suffolk

ISBN 0 571 08540 7

Contents

Microcosmos

I am that fantasy which race has wrought
Of mundane chance-material. I am time
Paeaned by the senses five like bells that chime.

I am that cramped and crumbling house of clay
Where mansoul weaves the secret webs of thought.
Venturer — automaton — I cannot tell
What powers and instincts animate and betray
And do their dreamwork in me. Seed and star,
Sown by the wind, in spirit I am far
From self, the dull control with whom I dwell.

Also I am ancestral. Aeons ahead
And ages back, both son and sire I live
Mote-like between the unquickened and the dead —
From whom I take, and unto whom I give.

The Old Huntsman

I've never ceased to curse the day I signed
A seven years' bargain for the Golden Fleece.
'Twas a bad deal all round; and dear enough
It cost me, what with my daft management,
And the mean folk as owed and never paid me,
And backing losers; and the local bucks
Egging me on with whiskys while I bragged
The man I was when huntsman to the Squire.

I'd have been prosperous if I'd took a farm
Of fifty acres, drove my gig and haggled
At Monday markets; now I've squandered all
My savings; nigh three hundred pound I got
As testimonial when I'd grown too stiff
And slow to press a beaten fox.

The Fleece!

'Twas the damned Fleece that wore my Emily out,
The wife of thirty years who served me well;
(Not like this beldam clattering in the kitchen,
That never trims a lamp nor sweeps the floor,
And brings me greasy soup in a foul crock.)

Blast the old harridan! What's fetched her now,
Leaving me in the dark, and short of fire?
And where's my pipe? 'Tis lucky I've a turn
For thinking, and remembering all that's past.
And now's my hour, before I hobble to bed,
To set the works a-wheezing, wind the clock
That keeps the time of life with feeble tick
Behind my bleared old face that stares and wonders.

.   .   .   .

It's queer how, in the dark, comes back to mind
Some morning of September. We've been digging
In a steep sandy warren, riddled with holes,
And I've just pulled the terrier out and left
A sharp-nosed cub-face blinking there and snapping,
Then in a moment seen him mobbed and torn
To strips in the baying hurly of the pack.
I picture it so clear: the dusty sunshine
On bracken, and the men with spades, that wipe
Red faces: one tilts up a mug of ale.
And, having stopped to clean my gory hands,
I whistle the jostling beauties out of the wood.

I'm but a daft old fool! I often wish
The Squire were back again — ah! he was a man!
They don't breed men like him these days; he'd come
For sure, and sit and talk and suck his briar
Till the old wife brings up a dish of tea.

Ay, those were days, when I was serving Squire!
I never knowed such sport as '85,
The winter afore the one that snowed us silly.

.   .   .   .

Once in a way the parson will drop in
And read a bit o' the Bible, if I'm bad,
And pray the Lord to make my spirit whole
In faith: he leaves some 'baccy on the shelf,
And wonders I don't keep a dog to cheer me
Because he knows I'm mortal fond of dogs!

I ask you, what's a gent like that to me
As wouldn't know Elijah if I saw him,
Nor have the wit to keep him on the talk?
'Tis kind of parson to be troubling still
With such as me; but he's a town-bred chap,
Full of his college notions and Christmas hymns.

Religion beats me. I'm amazed at folk
Drinking the gospels in and never scratching
Their heads for questions. When I was a lad
I learned a bit from mother, and never thought
To educate myself for prayers and psalms.

But now I'm old and bald and serious-minded,
With days to sit and ponder. I'd no chance
When young and gay to get the hang of all
This Hell and Heaven: and when the clergy hoick
And holloa from their pulpits, I'm asleep,
However hard I listen; and when they pray
It seems we're all like children sucking sweets
In school, and wondering whether master sees.

I used to dream of Hell when I was first
Promoted to a huntsman's job, and scent
Was rotten, and all the foxes disappeared,
And hounds were short of blood; and officers

From barracks over-rode 'em all day long
On weedy, whistling nags that knocked a hole
In every fence; good sportsmen to a man
And brigadiers by now, but dreadful hard
On a young huntsman keen to show some sport.

Ay, Hell was thick with captains, and I rode
The lumbering brute that's beat in half a mile,
And blunders into every blind old ditch.
Hell was the coldest scenting land I've known,
And both my whips were always lost, and hounds
Would never get their heads down; and a man
On a great yawing chestnut trying to cast 'em
While I was in a corner pounded by
The ugliest hog-backed stile you've clapped your eyes on.
There was an iron-spiked fence round all the coverts,
And civil-spoken keepers I couldn't trust,
And the main earth unstopp'd. The fox I found
Was always a three-legged 'un from a bag,
Who reeked of aniseed and wouldn't run.
The farmers were all ploughing their old pasture
And bellowing at me when I rode their beans
To cast for beaten fox, or galloped on
With hounds to a lucky view. I'd lost my voice
Although I shouted fit to burst my guts,
And couldn't blow my horn.

                              And when I woke,
Emily snored, and barn-cocks started crowing,
And morn was at the window; and I was glad
To be alive because I heard the cry
Of hounds like church-bells chiming on a Sunday.
Ay, that's the song I'd wish to hear in Heaven!
The cry of hounds was Heaven for me: I know
Parson would call me crazed and wrong to say it,
But where's the use of life and being glad
If God's not in your gladness?

I've no brains
For book-learned studies; but I've heard men say
There's much in print that clergy have to wink at:
Though many I've met were jolly chaps, and rode
To hounds, and walked me puppies; and could pick
Good legs and loins and necks and shoulders, ay,
And feet — 'twas necks and feet I looked at first.

Some hounds I've known were wise as half your saints,
And better hunters. That old dog of the Duke's,
Harlequin; what a dog he was to draw!
And what a note he had, and what a nose
When foxes ran down wind and scent was catchy!
And that light lemon bitch of the Squire's, old Dorcas —
She were a marvellous hunter, were old Dorcas!
Ay, oft I've thought, 'If there were hounds in Heaven,
With God as master, taking no subscription;
And all His blessèd country farmed by tenants,
And a straight-necked old fox in every gorse!'
But when I came to work it out, I found
There'd be too many huntsmen wanting places,
Though some I've known might get a job with Nick!

. . . .

I've come to think of God as something like
The figure of a man the old Duke was
When I was turning hounds to Nimrod King,
Before his Grace was took so bad with gout
And had to quit the saddle. Tall and spare,
Clean-shaved and grey, with shrewd, kind eyes, that twinkled,
And easy walk; who, when he gave good words,
Gave them whole-hearted; and would never blame
Without just cause. Lord God might be like that,
Sitting alone in a great room of books
Some evening after hunting.

Now I'm tired
With hearkening to the tick-tack on the shelf;
And pondering makes me doubtful.

Riding home
On a moonless night of cloud that feels like frost
Though stars are hidden (hold your feet up, horse!)
And thinking what a task I had to draw
A pack with all those lame 'uns, and the lot
Wanting a rest from all this open weather;
That's what I'm doing now.

And likely, too,
The frost'll be a long 'un, and the night
One sleep. The parsons say we'll wake to find
A country blinding-white with dazzle of snow.

The naked stars make men feel lonely, wheeling
And glinting on the puddles in the road.
And then you listen to the wind, and wonder
If folk are quite such bucks as they appear
When dressed by London tailors, looking down
Their boots at covert side, and thinking big.

.   .   .   .   .

This world's a funny place to live in. Soon
I'll need to change my country; but I know
'Tis little enough I've understood my life,
And a power of sights I've missed, and foreign marvels.

I used to feel it, riding on spring days
In meadows pied with sun and chasing clouds,
And half forget how I was there to catch
The foxes; lose the angry, eager feeling
A huntsman ought to have, that's out for blood,
And means his hounds to get it!

                              Now I know
It's God that speaks to us when we're bewitched,
Smelling the hay in June and smiling quiet;
Or when there's been a spell of summer drought,
Lying awake and listening to the rain.

                •   •   •   •

I'd like to be the simpleton I was
In the old days when I was whipping-in
To a little harrier-pack in Worcestershire,
And loved a dairymaid, but never knew it
Until she'd wed another. So I've loved
My life; and when the good years are gone down,
Discover what I've lost.

                              I never broke
Out of my blundering self into the world,
But let it all go past me, like a man
Half asleep in a land that's full of wars.

What a grand thing 'twould be if I could go
Back to the kennels now and take my hounds
For summer exercise; be riding out
With forty couple when the quiet skies
Are streaked with sunrise, and the silly birds
Grown hoarse with singing; cobwebs on the furze
Up on the hill, and all the country strange,
With no one stirring; and the horses fresh,
Sniffing the air I'll never breathe again.

                •   •   •   •

You've brought the lamp, then, Martha? I've no mind
For newspaper to-night, nor bread and cheese.
Give me the candle, and I'll get to bed.

Absolution

The anguish of the earth absolves our eyes
Till beauty shines in all that we can see.
War is our scourge; yet war has made us wise,
And, fighting for our freedom, we are free.

Horror of wounds and anger at the foe,
And loss of things desired; all these must pass.
We are the happy legion, for we know
Time's but a golden wind that shakes the grass.

There was an hour when we were loth to part
From life we longed to share no less than others.
Now, having claimed this heritage of heart,
What need we more, my comrades and my brothers?

To My Brother

Give me your hand, my brother, search my face;
Look in these eyes lest I should think of shame;
For we have made an end of all things base.
We are returning by the road we came.

Your lot is with the ghosts of soldiers dead,
And I am in the field where men must fight.
But in the gloom I see your laurell'd head
And through your victory I shall win the light.

When I'm among a Blaze of Lights

When I'm among a blaze of lights,
With tawdry music and cigars
And women dawdling through delights,
And officers in cocktail bars,

Sometimes I think of garden nights
And elm trees nodding at the stars.

I dream of a small firelit room
With yellow candles burning straight,
And glowing pictures in the gloom,
And kindly books that hold me late.
Of things like these I choose to think
When I can never be alone:
Then someone says 'Another drink?'
And turns my living heart to stone.

Golgotha

Through darkness curves a spume of falling flares
That flood the field with shallow, blanching light.
   The huddled sentry stares
    On gloom at war with white,
     And white receding slow, submerged in gloom.
     Guns into mimic thunder burst and boom,
    And mirthless laughter rakes the whistling night.
The sentry keeps his watch where no one stirs
But the brown rats, the nimble scavengers.

The Redeemer

Darkness: the rain sluiced down; the mire was deep;
It was past twelve on a mid-winter night,
When peaceful folk in beds lay snug asleep;
There, with much work to do before the light,
We lugged our clay-sucked boots as best we might
Along the trench; sometimes a bullet sang,
And droning shells burst with a hollow bang;
We were soaked, chilled and wretched, every one;
Darkness; the distant wink of a huge gun.

I turned in the black ditch, loathing the storm;
A rocket fizzed and burned with blanching flare,
And lit the face of what had been a form
Floundering in mirk. He stood before me there;
I say that He was Christ; stiff in the glare,
And leaning forward from His burdening task,
Both arms supporting it; His eyes on mine
Stared from the woeful head that seemed a mask
Of mortal pain in Hell's unholy shine.

No thorny crown, only a woollen cap
He wore — an English soldier, white and strong,
Who loved his time like any simple chap,
Good days of work and sport and homely song;
Now he has learned that nights are very long,
And dawn a watching of the windowed sky.
But to the end, unjudging, he'll endure
Horror and pain, not uncontent to die
That Lancaster on Lune may stand secure.

He faced me, reeling in his weariness,
Shouldering his load of planks, so hard to bear.
I say that He was Christ, who wrought to bless
All groping things with freedom bright as air,
And with His mercy washed and made them fair.
Then the flame sank, and all grew black as pitch,
While we began to struggle along the ditch;
And someone flung his burden in the muck,
Mumbling: 'O Christ Almighty, now I'm stuck!'

In the Pink

So Davies wrote: 'This leaves me in the pink'.
Then scrawled his name: 'Your loving sweetheart, Willie'.
With crosses for a hug. He'd had a drink
Of rum and tea; and, though the barn was chilly,
For once his blood ran warm; he had pay to spend.
Winter was passing; soon the year would mend.

But he couldn't sleep that night; stiff in the dark
He groaned and thought of Sundays at the farm,
And how he'd go as cheerful as a lark
In his best suit, to wander arm in arm
With brown-eyed Gwen, and whisper in her ear
The simple, silly things she liked to hear.

And then he thought: to-morrow night we trudge
Up to the trenches, and my boots are rotten.
Five miles of stodgy clay and freezing sludge,
And everything but wretchedness forgotten.
To-night he's in the pink; but soon he'll die.
And still the war goes on — *he* don't know why.

'Blighters'

The House is crammed: tier beyond tier they grin
And cackle at the Show, while prancing ranks
Of harlots shrill the chorus, drunk with din;
'We're sure the Kaiser loves our dear old Tanks!'

I'd like to see a Tank come down the stalls,
Lurching to rag-time tunes, or 'Home, sweet Home',
And there'd be no more jokes in Music-halls
To mock the riddled corpses round Bapaume.

At Carnoy

Down in the hollow there's the whole Brigade
Camped in four groups: through twilight falling slow
I hear a sound of mouth-organs, ill-played,
And murmur of voices, gruff, confused, and low.
Crouched among thistle-tufts I've watched the glow
Of a blurred orange sunset flare and fade;
And I'm content. To-morrow we must go
To take some cursèd Wood . . . O world God made!

July 3rd, 1916.

'They'

The Bishop tells us: 'When the boys come back
'They will not be the same; for they'll have fought
'In a just cause: they lead the last attack
'On Anti-Christ; their comrades' blood has bought
'New right to breed an honourable race,
'They have challenged Death and dared him face to face.'

'We're none of us the same!' the boys reply.
'For George lost both his legs; and Bill's stone blind;
'Poor Jim's shot through the lungs and like to die;
'And Bert's gone syphilitic: you'll not find
'A chap who's served that hasn't found *some* change.'
And the Bishop said: 'The ways of God are strange!'

Stand-to: Good Friday Morning

I'd been on duty from two till four.
I went and stared at the dug-out door.
Down in the frowst I heard them snore.
'Stand to!' Somebody grunted and swore.
  Dawn was misty; the skies were still;
  Larks were singing, discordant, shrill;
  They seemed happy; but *I* felt ill.
Deep in water I splashed my way
Up the trench to our bogged front line.
Rain had fallen the whole damned night.
O Jesus, send me a wound to-day,
And I'll believe in Your bread and wine,
And get my bloody old sins washed white!

The One-Legged Man

Propped on a stick he viewed the August weald;
Squat orchard trees and oasts with painted cowls;
A homely, tangled hedge, a corn-stalked field,
And sound of barking dogs and farmyard fowls.

And he'd come home again to find it more
Desirable than ever it was before.
How right it seemed that he should reach the span
Of comfortable years allowed to man!
Splendid to eat and sleep and choose a wife,
Safe with his wound, a citizen of life.
He hobbled blithely through the garden gate,
And thought: 'Thank God they had to amputate!'

Died of Wounds

His wet white face and miserable eyes
Brought nurses to him more than groans and sighs:

But hoarse and low and rapid rose and fell
His troubled voice: he did the business well.

The ward grew dark; but he was still complaining
And calling out for 'Dickie'. 'Curse the Wood!
'It's time to go. O Christ, and what's the good?
'We'll never take it, and it's always raining.'

I wondered where he'd been; then heard him shout,
'They snipe like hell! O Dickie, don't go out' . . .
I fell asleep . . . Next morning he was dead;
And some Slight Wound lay smiling on the bed.

Before the Battle

Music of whispering trees
Hushed by a broad-winged breeze
Where shaken water gleams;
And evening radiance falling
With reedy bird-notes calling.
O bear me safe through dark, you low-voiced streams.

I have no need to pray
That fear may pass away;
I scorn the growl and rumble of the fight
That summons me from cool
Silence of marsh and pool
And yellow lilies islanded in light.
O river of stars and shadows, lead me through the night.

June 25th, 1916.

Before Day

Come in this hour to set my spirit free
When earth is no more mine though night goes out,

And stretching forth these arms I cannot be
Lord of winged sunrise and dim Arcady:
When fieldward boys far off with clack and shout
From orchards scare the birds in sudden rout,
Come, ere my heart grows cold and full of doubt,
In the still summer dawns that waken me.

When the first lark goes up to look for day
And morning glimmers out of dreams, come then
Out of the songless valleys, over grey
Wide misty lands to bring me on my way:
For I am lone, a dweller among men
Hungered for what my heart shall never say.

Prelude: The Troops

Dim, gradual thinning of the shapeless gloom
Shudders to drizzling daybreak that reveals
Disconsolate men who stamp their sodden boots
And turn dulled, sunken faces to the sky
Haggard and hopeless. They, who have beaten down
The stale despair of night, must now renew
Their desolation in the truce of dawn,
Murdering the livid hours that grope for peace.

Yet these, who cling to life with stubborn hands,
Can grin through storms of death and find a gap
In the clawed, cruel tangles of his defence.
They march from safety, and the bird-sung joy
Of grass-green thickets, to the land where all
Is ruin, and nothing blossoms but the sky
That hastens over them where they endure
Sad, smoking, flat horizons, reeking woods,
And foundered trench-lines volleying doom for doom.

O my brave brown companions, when your souls
Flock silently away, and the eyeless dead

Shame the wild beast of battle on the ridge,
Death will stand grieving in that field of war
Since your unvanquished hardihood is spent.
And through some mooned Valhalla there will pass
Battalions and battalions, scarred from hell;
The unreturning army that was youth;
The legions who have suffered and are dust.

Counter-Attack

We'd gained our first objective hours before
While dawn broke like a face with blinking eyes,
Pallid, unshaved and thirsty, blind with smoke.
Things seemed all right at first. We held their line,
With bombers posted, Lewis guns well placed,
And clink of shovels deepening the shallow trench.
  The place was rotten with dead; green clumsy legs
  High-booted, sprawled and grovelled along the saps;
  And trunks, face downward, in the sucking mud,
  Wallowed like trodden sand-bags loosely filled;
  And naked sodden buttocks, mats of hair,
  Bulged, clotted heads slept in the plastering slime.
  And then the rain began, — the jolly old rain!

A yawning soldier knelt against the bank,
Staring across the morning blear with fog;
He wondered when the Allemands would get busy;
And then, of course, they started with five-nines
Traversing, sure as fate, and never a dud.
Mute in the clamour of shells he watched them burst
Spouting dark earth and wire with gusts from hell,
While posturing giants dissolved in drifts of smoke.
He crouched and flinched, dizzy with galloping fear,
Sick for escape, — loathing the strangled horror
And butchered, frantic gestures of the dead.

An officer came blundering down the trench:
'Stand-to and man the fire-step!' On he went ...
Gasping and bawling, 'Fire-step ... counter-attack!'
  Then the haze lifted. Bombing on the right
  Down the old sap: machine-guns on the left;
  And stumbling figures looming out in front.
  'O Christ, they're coming at us!' Bullets spat,
And he remembered his rifle ... rapid fire ...
And started blazing wildly ... then a bang
Crumpled and spun him sideways, knocked him out
To grunt and wriggle: none heeded him; he choked
And fought the flapping veils of smothering gloom,
Lost in a blurred confusion of yells and groans ...
Down, and down, and down, he sank and drowned,
Bleeding to death. The counter-attack had failed.

The Rear-Guard

(HINDENBURG LINE, APRIL 1917)

Groping along the tunnel, step by step,
He winked his prying torch with patching glare
From side to side, and sniffed the unwholesome air.

Tins, boxes, bottles, shapes too vague to know;
A mirror smashed, the mattress from a bed;
And he, exploring fifty feet below
The rosy gloom of battle overhead.

Tripping, he grabbed the wall; saw some one lie
Humped at his feet, half-hidden by a rug,
And stooped to give the sleeper's arm a tug.
'I'm looking for headquarters.' No reply.
'God blast your neck!' (For days he'd had no sleep,)
'Get up and guide me through this stinking place.'

Savage, he kicked a soft, unanswering heap,
And flashed his beam across the livid face

Terribly glaring up, whose eyes yet wore
Agony dying hard ten days before;
And fists of fingers clutched a blackening wound.

Alone he staggered on until he found
Dawn's ghost that filtered down a shafted stair
To the dazed, muttering creatures underground
Who hear the boom of shells in muffled sound.
At last, with sweat of horror in his hair,
He climbed through darkness to the twilight air,
Unloading hell behind him step by step.

Attack

At dawn the ridge emerges massed and dun
In the wild purple of the glow'ring sun,
Smouldering through spouts of drifting smoke that shroud
The menacing scarred slope; and, one by one,
Tanks creep and topple forward to the wire.
The barrage roars and lifts. Then, clumsily bowed
With bombs and guns and shovels and battle-gear,
Men jostle and climb to meet the bristling fire.
Lines of grey, muttering faces, masked with fear,
They leave their trenches, going over the top,
While time ticks blank and busy on their wrists,
And hope, with furtive eyes and grappling fists,
Flounders in mud. O Jesus, make it stop!

Dreamers

Soldiers are citizens of death's grey land,
    Drawing no dividend from time's to-morrows.
In the great hour of destiny they stand,
    Each with his feuds, and jealousies, and sorrows.
Soldiers are sworn to action; they must win
    Some flaming, fatal climax with their lives.

Soldiers are dreamers; when the guns begin
    They think of firelit homes, clean beds and wives.

I see them in foul dug-outs, gnawed by rats,
    And in the ruined trenches, lashed with rain,
Dreaming of things they did with balls and bats,
    And mocked by hopeless longing to regain
Bank-holidays, and picture shows, and spats,
    And going to the office in the train.

Twelve Months After

Hullo! here's my platoon, the lot I had last year.
'The war'll be over soon.'
                    'What 'opes?'
                                'No bloody fear!'
Then, 'Number Seven, 'shun! All present and correct.'
They're standing in the sun, impassive and erect.
Young Gibson with his grin; and Morgan, tired and white;
Jordan, who's out to win a D.C.M. some night;
And Hughes that's keen on wiring; and Davies ('79),
Who always must be firing at the Boche front line.

        .   .   .   .

'Old soldiers never die; they simply fide a-why!'
That's what they used to sing along the roads last spring;
That's what they used to say before the push began;
That's where they are to-day, knocked over to a man.

Base Details

If I were fierce, and bald, and short of breath,
    I'd live with scarlet Majors at the Base,
And speed glum heroes up the line to death.
    You'd see me with my puffy petulant face,

Guzzling and gulping in the best hotel,
  Reading the Roll of Honour. 'Poor young chap,'
I'd say — 'I used to know his father well;
  Yes, we've lost heavily in this last scrap.'
And when the war is done and youth stone dead,
I'd toddle safely home and die — in bed.

The General

'Good-morning; good-morning!' the General said
When we met him last week on our way to the line.
Now the soldiers he smiled at are most of 'em dead,
And we're cursing his staff for incompetent swine.
'He's a cheery old card,' grunted Harry to Jack
As they slogged up to Arras with rifle and pack.

.   .   .

But he did for them both by his plan of attack.

Lamentations

I found him in the guard-room at the Base.
From the blind darkness I had heard his crying
And blundered in. With puzzled, patient face
A sergeant watched him; it was no good trying
To stop it; for he howled and beat his chest.
And, all because his brother had gone west,
Raved at the bleeding war; his rampant grief
Moaned, shouted, sobbed, and choked, while he was kneeling
Half-naked on the floor. In my belief
Such men have lost all patriotic feeling.

Does it Matter?

Does it matter? — losing your legs? . . .
For people will always be kind,

And you need not show that you mind
When the others come in after hunting
To gobble their muffins and eggs.

Does it matter? — losing your sight? . . .
There's such splendid work for the blind;
And people will always be kind,
As you sit on the terrace remembering
And turning your face to the light.

Do they matter? — those dreams from the pit? . . .
You can drink and forget and be glad,
And people won't say that you're mad;
For they'll know you've fought for your country
And no one will worry a bit.

Fight to a Finish

The boys came back. Bands played and flags were flying,
    And Yellow-Pressmen thronged the sunlit street
To cheer the soldiers who'd refrained from dying,
    And hear the music of returning feet.
'Of all the thrills and ardours War has brought,
This moment is the finest.' (So they thought.)

Snapping their bayonets on to charge the mob,
    Grim Fusiliers broke ranks with glint of steel.
At last the boys had found a cushy job.

· · · ·

    I heard the Yellow-Pressmen grunt and squeal;
And with my trusty bombers turned and went
To clear those Junkers out of Parliament.

Suicide in the Trenches

I knew a simple soldier boy
Who grinned at life in empty joy,
Slept soundly through the lonesome dark,
And whistled early with the lark.

In winter trenches, cowed and glum,
With crumps and lice and lack of rum,
He put a bullet through his brain.
No one spoke of him again.

.   .   .   .

You smug-faced crowds with kindling eye
Who cheer when soldier lads march by,
Sneak home and pray you'll never know
The hell where youth and laughter go.

Glory of Women

You love us when we're heroes, home on leave,
Or wounded in a mentionable place.
You worship decorations; you believe
That chivalry redeems the war's disgrace.
You make us shells. You listen with delight,
By tales of dirt and danger fondly thrilled.
You crown our distant ardours while we fight,
And mourn our laurelled memories when we're killed.
You can't believe that British troops 'retire'
When hell's last horror breaks them, and they run,
Trampling the terrible corpses — blind with blood.
  O German mother dreaming by the fire,
    While you are knitting socks to send your son
    His face is trodden deeper in the mud.

Trench Duty

Shaken from sleep, and numbed and scarce awake,
Out in the trench with three hours' watch to take,
I blunder through the splashing mirk; and then
Hear the gruff muttering voices of the men
Crouching in cabins candle-chinked with light.
Hark! There's the big bombardment on our right
Rumbling and bumping; and the dark's a glare
Of flickering horror in the sectors where
We raid the Boche; men waiting, stiff and chilled,
Or crawling on their bellies through the wire.
'What? Stretcher-bearers wanted? Some one killed?'
Five minutes ago I heard a sniper fire:
Why did he do it? . . . Starlight overhead —
Blank stars. I'm wide-awake; and some chap's dead.

To Any Dead Officer

Well, how are things in Heaven? I wish you'd say,
   Because I'd like to know that you're all right.
Tell me, have you found everlasting day,
   Or been sucked in by everlasting night?
For when I shut my eyes your face shows plain;
   I hear you make some cheery old remark —
I can rebuild you in my brain,
   Though you've gone out patrolling in the dark.

You hated tours of trenches; you were proud
   Of nothing more than having good years to spend;
Longed to get home and join the careless crowd
   Of chaps who work in peace with Time for friend.
That's all washed out now. You're beyond the wire:
   No earthly chance can send you crawling back;
You've finished with machine-gun fire —
   Knocked over in a hopeless dud-attack.

Somehow I always thought you'd get done in,
    Because you were so desperate keen to live:
You were all out to try and save your skin,
    Well knowing how much the world had got to give.
You joked at shells and talked the usual 'shop,'
    Stuck to your dirty job and did it fine:
With 'Jesus Christ! when *will* it stop?
    Three years . . . It's hell unless we break their line.'

So when they told me you'd been left for dead
    I wouldn't believe them, feeling it *must* be true.
Next week the bloody Roll of Honour said
    'Wounded and missing' — (That's the thing to do
When lads are left in shell-holes dying slow,
    With nothing but blank sky and wounds that ache,
Moaning for water till they know
    It's night, and then it's not worth while to wake!)

.   .   .   .

Good-bye, old lad! Remember me to God,
    And tell Him that our Politicians swear
They won't give in till Prussian Rule's been trod
    Under the Heel of England . . . Are you there? . . .
Yes . . . and the War won't end for at least two years;
But we've got stacks of men . . . I'm blind with tears,
    Staring into the dark. Cheero!
I wish they'd killed you in a decent show.

Sick Leave

When I'm asleep, dreaming and lulled and warm, —
They come, the homeless ones, the noiseless dead.
While the dim charging breakers of the storm
Bellow and drone and rumble overhead,
Out of the gloom they gather about my bed.
    They whisper to my heart; their thoughts are mine.
    'Why are you here with all your watches ended?

From Ypres to Frise we sought you in the Line.'
In bitter safety I awake, unfriended;
And while the dawn begins with slashing rain
I think of the Battalion in the mud.
'When are you going out to them again?
Are they not still your brothers through our blood?'

Banishment

I am banished from the patient men who fight.
They smote my heart to pity, built my pride.
Shoulder to aching shoulder, side by side,
They trudged away from life's broad wealds of light.
Their wrongs were mine; and ever in my sight
They went arrayed in honour. But they died, —
Not one by one: and mutinous I cried
To those who sent them out into the night.

The darkness tells how vainly I have striven
To free them from the pit where they must dwell
In outcast gloom convulsed and jagged and riven
By grappling guns. Love drove me to rebel.
Love drives me back to grope with them through hell;
And in their tortured eyes I stand forgiven.

Thrushes

Tossed on the glittering air they soar and skim,
Whose voices make the emptiness of light
A windy palace. Quavering from the brim
Of dawn, and bold with song at edge of night,
They clutch their leafy pinnacles and sing
Scornful of man, and from his toils aloof
Whose heart's a haunted woodland whispering;
Whose thoughts return on tempest-baffled wing;
Who hears the cry of God in everything,
And storms the gate of nothingness for proof.

Autumn

October's bellowing anger breaks and cleaves
The bronzed battalions of the stricken wood
In whose lament I hear a voice that grieves
For battle's fruitless harvest, and the feud
Of outraged men. Their lives are like the leaves
Scattered in flocks of ruin, tossed and blown
Along the westering furnace flaring red.
O martyred youth and manhood overthrown,
The burden of your wrongs is on my head.

Invocation

Come down from heaven to meet me when my breath
Chokes, and through drumming shafts of stifling death
I stumble toward escape, to find the door
Opening on morn where I may breathe once more
Clear cock-crow airs across some valley dim
With whispering trees. While dawn along the rim
Of night's horizon flows in lakes of fire,
Come down from heaven's bright hill, my song's desire.

Belov'd and faithful, teach my soul to wake
In glades deep-ranked with flowers that gleam and shake
And flock your paths with wonder. In your gaze
Show me the vanquished vigil of my days.
Mute in that golden silence hung with green,
Come down from heaven and bring me in your eyes
Remembrance of all beauty that has been,
And stillness from the pools of Paradise.

Survivors

No doubt they'll soon get well; the shock and strain
Have caused their stammering, disconnected talk.

Of course they're 'longing to go out again,' —
    These boys with old, scared faces, learning to walk.
They'll soon forget their haunted nights; their cowed
    Subjection to the ghosts of friends who died, —
Their dreams that drip with murder; and they'll be proud
    Of glorious war that shatter'd all their pride . . .
Men who went out to battle, grim and glad;
Children, with eyes that hate you, broken and mad.

Craiglockart, October 1917.

Remorse

Lost in the swamp and welter of the pit,
He flounders off the duck-boards; only he knows
Each flash and spouting crash, — each instant lit
When gloom reveals the streaming rain. He goes
Heavily, blindly on. And, while he blunders,
'Could anything be worse than this?' — he wonders,
Remembering how he saw those Germans run,
Screaming for mercy among the stumps of trees:
Green-faced, they dodged and darted: there was one
Livid with terror, clutching at his knees . . .
Our chaps were sticking 'em like pigs . . . 'O hell!'
He thought — 'there's things in war one dare not tell
Poor father sitting safe at home, who reads
Of dying heroes and their deathless deeds.'

Dead Musicians

I

From you, Beethoven, Bach, Mozart,
    The substance of my dreams took fire.
You built cathedrals in my heart,
    And lit my pinnacled desire.

You were the ardour and the bright
   Procession of my thoughts toward prayer.
You were the wrath of storm, the light
   On distant citadels aflare.

II

Great names, I cannot find you now
   In these loud years of youth that strives
Through doom toward peace: upon my brow
   I wear a wreath of banished lives.
You have no part with lads who fought
   And laughed and suffered at my side.
Your fugues and symphonies have brought
   No memory of my friends who died.

III

For when my brain is on their track,
In slangy speech I call them back.
With fox-trot tunes their ghosts I charm.
'*Another little drink won't do us any harm.*'
   I think of rag-time; a bit of rag-time;
   And see their faces crowding round
   To the sound of the syncopated beat.
   They've got such jolly things to tell,
   Home from hell with a Blighty wound so neat . . .

.   .   .   .

And so the song breaks off; and I'm alone.
They're dead . . . For God's sake stop that gramophone.

Together

Splashing along the boggy woods all day,
And over brambled hedge and holding clay,
   I shall not think of him:
But when the watery fields grow brown and dim,
And hounds have lost their fox, and horses tire,

34

I know that he'll be with me on my way
Home through the darkness to the evening fire.

He's jumped each stile along the glistening lanes;
His hand will be upon the mud-soaked reins;
Hearing the saddle creak,
He'll wonder if the frost will come next week.
I shall forget him in the morning light;
And while we gallop on he will not speak:
But at the stable-door he'll say good-night.

Reconciliation

When you are standing at your hero's grave,
Or near some homeless village where he died,
Remember, through your heart's rekindling pride,
The German soldiers who were loyal and brave.

Men fought like brutes; and hideous things were done;
And you have nourished hatred, harsh and blind.
But in that Golgotha perhaps you'll find
The mothers of the men who killed your son.

November 1918.

The Dug-Out

Why do you lie with your legs ungainly huddled,
And one arm bent across your sullen, cold,
Exhausted face? It hurts my heart to watch you,
Deep-shadow'd from the candle's guttering gold;
And you wonder why I shake you by the shoulder;
Drowsy, you mumble and sigh and turn your head . . .
You are too young to fall asleep for ever;
And when you sleep you remind me of the dead.

St Venant, July 1918.

I Stood With the Dead

I stood with the Dead, so forsaken and still:
When dawn was grey I stood with the Dead.
And my slow heart said, 'You must kill, you must kill:
'Soldier, soldier, morning is red'.

On the shapes of the slain in their crumpled disgrace
I stared for a while through the thin cold rain . . .
'O lad that I loved, there is rain on your face,
'And your eyes are blurred and sick like the plain.'

I stood with the Dead . . . They were dead; they were dead;
My heart and my head beat a march of dismay:
And gusts of the wind came dulled by the guns.
'Fall in!' I shouted; 'Fall in for your pay!'

Memorial Tablet

(GREAT WAR)

Squire nagged and bullied till I went to fight,
(Under Lordy Derby's Scheme). I died in hell —
(They called it Passchendaele). My wound was slight,
And I was hobbling back; and then a shell
Burst slick upon the duck-boards: so I fell
Into the bottomless mud, and lost the light.

At sermon-time, while Squire is in his pew,
He gives my gilded name a thoughtful stare;
For, though low down upon the list, I'm there;
'In proud and glorious memory' . . . that's my due.
Two bleeding years I fought in France, for Squire:
I suffered anguish that he's never guessed.
Once I came home on leave: and then went west . . .
What greater glory could a man desire?

Memory

When I was young my heart and head were light,
And I was gay and feckless as a colt
Out in the fields, with morning in the may,
Wind on the grass, wings in the orchard bloom.
  O thrilling sweet, my joy, when life was free
  And all the paths led on from hawthorn-time
  Across the carolling meadows into June.

But now my heart is heavy-laden. I sit
Burning my dreams away beside the fire:
For death has made me wise and bitter and strong;
And I am rich in all that I have lost.
  O starshine on the fields of long-ago,
  Bring me the darkness and the nightingale;
  Dim wealds of vanished summer, peace of home,
  And silence; and the faces of my friends.

Elegy

(TO ROBERT ROSS)

Your dextrous wit will haunt us long
Wounding our grief with yesterday.
Your laughter is a broken song;
And death has found you, kind and gay.

We may forget those transient things
That made your charm and our delight:
But loyal love has deathless wings
That rise and triumph out of night.

So, in the days to come, your name
Shall be as music that ascends
When honour turns a heart from shame . . .
O heart of hearts! . . . O friend of friends!

Ancient History

Adam, a brown old vulture in the rain,
Shivered below his wind-whipped olive-trees;
Huddling sharp chin on scarred and scraggy knees,
He moaned and mumbled to his darkening brain;
'*He was the grandest of them all — was Cain!*
'A lion laired in the hills, that none could tire;
'Swift as a stag; a stallion of the plain,
'Hungry and fierce with deeds of huge desire.'

Grimly he thought of Abel, soft and fair —
A lover with disaster in his face,
And scarlet blossom twisted in bright hair.
'Afraid to fight; was murder more disgrace? . . .
'*God always hated Cain*' . . . He bowed his head —
The gaunt wild man whose lovely sons were dead.

Idyll

In the grey summer garden I shall find you
With day-break and the morning hills behind you.
There will be rain-wet roses; stir of wings;
And down the wood a thrush that wakes and sings.
Not from the past you'll come, but from that deep
Where beauty murmurs to the soul asleep:
And I shall know the sense of life re-born
From dreams into the mystery of morn
Where gloom and brightness meet. And standing there
Till that calm song is done, at last we'll share
The league-spread, quiring symphonies that are
Joy in the world, and peace, and dawn's one star.

Lovers

You were glad to-night: and now you've gone away.
Flushed in the dark, you put your dreams to bed;

But as you fall asleep I hear you say
Those tired sweet drowsy words we left unsaid.

Sleep well: for I can follow you, to bless
And lull your distant beauty where you roam;
And with wild songs of hoarded loveliness
Recall you to these arms that were your home.

Slumber-Song

Sleep; and my song shall build about your bed
A paradise of dimness. You shall feel
The folding of tired wings; and peace will dwell
Throned in your silence: and one hour shall hold
Summer, and midnight, and immensity
Lulled to forgetfulness. For, where you dream,
The stately gloom of foliage shall embower
Your slumbering thought with tapestries of blue.
And there shall be no memory of the sky,
Nor sunlight with its cruelty of swords.
But, to your soul that sinks from deep to deep
Through drowned and glimmering colour, Time shall be
Only slow rhythmic swaying; and your breath;
And roses in the darkness; and my love.

Vision

I love all things that pass: their briefness is
Music that fades on transient silences.
Winds, birds, and glittering leaves that flare and fall —
They fling delight across the world; they call
To rhythmic-flashing limbs that rove and race . . .
    A moment in the dawn for Youth's lit face;
    A moment's passion, closing on the cry —
    'O Beauty, born of lovely things that die!'

39

Aftermath

*H*ave you forgotten yet? . . .
For the world's events have rumbled on since those gagged days,
Like traffic checked while at the crossing of city-ways:
And the haunted gap in your mind has filled with thoughts that
    flow
Like clouds in the lit heaven of life; and you're a man reprieved to
    go,
Taking your peaceful share of Time, with joy to spare.
But the past is just the same — and War's a bloody game . . .
Have you forgotten yet? . . .
Look down, and swear by the slain of the War that you'll never forget.

Do you remember the dark months you held the sector at
    Mametz —
The nights you watched and wired and dug and piled sandbags on
    parapets?
Do you remember the rats; and the stench
Of corpses rotting in front of the front-line trench —
And dawn coming, dirty-white, and chill with a hopeless rain?
Do you ever stop and ask, 'Is it all going to happen again?'

Do you remember that hour of din before the attack —
And the anger, the blind compassion that seized and shook you
    then
As you peered at the doomed and haggard faces of your men?
Do you remember the stretcher-cases lurching back
With dying eyes and lolling heads — those ashen-grey
Masks of the lads who once were keen and kind and gay?

Have you forgotten yet? . . .
Look up, and swear by the green of the spring that you'll never forget.

March 1919.

Falling Asleep

Voices moving about in the quiet house:
Thud of feet and a muffled shutting of doors:
Everyone yawning. Only the clocks are alert.

Out in the night there's autumn-smelling gloom
Crowded with whispering trees; across the park
A hollow cry of hounds like lonely bells:
And I know that the clouds are moving across the moon;
The low, red, rising moon. Now herons call
And wrangle by their pool; and hooting owls
Sail from the wood above pale stooks of oats.

Waiting for sleep, I drift from thoughts like these;
And where to-day was dream-like, build my dreams.
Music . . . there was a bright white room below,
And someone singing a song about a soldier,
One hour, two hours ago: and soon the song
Will be 'last night': but now the beauty swings
Across my brain, ghost of remembered chords
Which still can make such radiance in my dream
That I can watch the marching of my soldiers,
And count their faces; faces; sunlit faces.

Falling asleep . . . the herons, and the hounds. . . .
September in the darkness; and the world
I've known; all fading past me into peace.

Everyone Sang

Everyone suddenly burst out singing;
And I was filled with such delight
As prisoned birds must find in freedom,
Winging wildly across the white
Orchards and dark-green fields; on — on — and out of sight.

Everyone's voice was suddenly lifted;
And beauty came like the setting sun:
My heart was shaken with tears; and horror
Drifted away . . . O, but Everyone
Was a bird; and the song was wordless; the singing will never be
    done.

On Reading the War Diary of a
Defunct Ambassador

So that's your Diary — that's your private mind
Translated into shirt-sleeved History. That
Is what diplomacy has left behind
For after-ages to peruse, and find
What passed beneath your elegant silk-hat.

You were a fine old gentleman; compact
Of shrewdness, charm, refinement and finesse.
Impeccable in breeding, taste and dress,
No diplomatic quality you lacked —
No tittle of ambassadorial tact.

I can imagine you among 'the guns',
Urbanely peppering partridge, grouse, or pheasant —
Guest of those infinitely privileged ones
Whose lives are padded, petrified, and pleasant.
I visualize you feeding off gold plate
And gossiping on grave affairs of State.

Now you're defunct; your gossip's gravely printed;
The world discovers where you lunched and dined
On such and such a day; and what was hinted
By ministers and generals far behind
The all-important conflict, carnage-tinted.

The world can read the rumours that you gleaned
From various Fronts; the well-known Names you met;

Each conference you attended and convened;
And (at appropriate moments) what you ate.
Thus (if the world's acute) it can derive
Your self, exact, uncensored and alive.

The world will find no pity in your pages;
No exercise of spirit worthy of mention;
Only a public-funeral grief-convention;
And all the circumspection of the ages.
But I, for one, am grateful, overjoyed,
And unindignant that your punctual pen
Should have been so constructively employed
In manifesting to unprivileged men
The visionless officialized fatuity
That once kept Europe safe for Perpetuity.

Monody on the Demolition of Devonshire House

Strolling one afternoon along a street
Whose valuable vastness can compare
With anything on earth in the complete
Efficiency of its mammoniac air —
Strolling (to put it plainly) through those bits
Of Londonment adjacent to the Ritz,
(While musing on the social gap between
Myself, whose arrogance is mostly brainy,
And those whose pride, on sunlit days and rainy,
Must loll and glide in yacht and limousine),
Something I saw, beyond a boarded barrier,
Which manifested well that Time's no tarrier.

Where stood the low-built mansion, once so great,
Ducal, demure, secure in its estate —
Where Byron rang the bell and limped upstairs,
And Lord knows what political affairs

Got muddled and remodelled while Their Graces
Manned unperturbed Elizabethan faces —
There, blankly overlooked by wintry strange
Frontage of houses rawly-lit by change,
Industrious workmen reconstructed quite
The lumbered, pegged, and excavated site;
And not one nook survived to screen a mouse
In what was Devonshire (God rest it) House.

Villa d'Este Gardens

'Of course you saw the Villa d'Este Gardens,'
Writes one of my Italianistic friends.
Of course; of course; I saw them in October,
Spired with pinaceous ornamental gloom
Of that arboreal elegy the cypress.

Those fountains, too, 'like ghosts of cypresses'; —
(The phrase occurred to me while I was leaning
On an old balustrade; imbibing sunset;
Wrapped in my verse vocation) — how they linked me
With Byron, Landor, Liszt, and Robert Browning! . . .
A *Liebestraum* of Liszt cajoled my senses.

My language favoured Landor, chaste and formal.
My intellect (though slightly in abeyance)
Functioned against a Byronistic background.
Then Browning jogged my elbow; bade me hob-nob
With some forgotten painter of dim frescoes
That haunt the Villa's intramural twilight.

While roaming in the Villa d'Este Gardens
I felt like that . . . and fumbled for my note-book.

Concert-Interpretation

(LE SACRE DU PRINTEMPS)

The audience pricks an intellectual Ear ...
Stravinsky ... Quite the Concert of the Year!

Forgetting now that none-so-distant date
When they (or folk facsimilar in state
Of mind) first heard with hisses — hoots — guffaws —
This abstract Symphony (they booed because
Stravinsky jumped their Wagner palisade
With modes that seemed cacophonous and queer),
Forgetting now the hullabaloo they made,
The Audience pricks an intellectual ear.

Bassoons begin ... Sonority envelops
Our auditory innocence; and brings
To Me, I must admit, some drift of things
Omnific, seminal, and adolescent.
Polyphony through dissonance develops
A serpent-conscious Eden, crude but pleasant;
While vibro-atmospheric copulations
With mezzo-forte mysteries of noise
Prelude Stravinsky's statement of the joys
That unify the monkeydom of nations.

This matter is most indelicate indeed!
Yet one perceives no symptom of stampede.
The Stalls remain unruffled: craniums gleam:
Swept by a storm of pizzicato chords,
Elaborate ladies re-assure their lords
With lifting brows that signify 'Supreme!'
While orchestrated gallantry of goats
Impugns the astigmatic programme-notes.

In the Grand Circle one observes no sign
Of riot: peace prevails along the line.

45

And in the Gallery, cargoed to capacity,
No tremor bodes eruptions and alarms.
They are listening to this not-quite-new audacity
As though it were by someone dead, — like Brahms.

But savagery pervades Me; I am frantic
With corybantic rupturing of laws.
Come, dance, and seize this clamorous chance to function
Creatively, — abandoning compunction
In anti-social rhapsodic applause!
Lynch the conductor! Jugulate the drums!
Butcher the brass! Ensanguinate the strings!
Throttle the flutes!... Stravinsky's April comes
With pitiless pomp and pain of sacred springs...
Incendiarize the Hall with resinous fires
Of sacrificial fiddles scorched and snapping!...

Meanwhile the music blazes and expires;
And the delighted Audience is clapping.

Founder's Feast

Old as a toothless Regius Professor
Ebbed the Madeira wine. Loquacious graduates
Sipped it with sublimation. They'd been drinking
The health of ... was it Edward the Confessor?
A solemn banquet glowed in every cheek,
While nicotinean fumes befogged the roof
And the carved gallery where prim choristers
Sang like Pre-Raphaelite angels through the reek.

Gowns, rose and scarlet in flamingo ranks,
Adorned the dais that shone with ancient silver;
And guests of honour gazed far down the Hall
With precognition of returning thanks.
There beamed the urbanest Law-lord on the Bench,
Debating with the Provost (ceremonious

46

In flushed degrees of vintage scholarship),
The politics of Plato, — and the French.

But on the Provost's left, in gold and blue,
Sat ... O my God! ... great Major-General Bluff ...
Enough enough enough enough enough!

Sheldonian Soliloquy

(DURING BACH'S B MINOR MASS)

My music-loving Self this afternoon
(Clothed in the gilded surname of Sassoon)
Squats in the packed Sheldonian and observes
An intellectual bee-hive perched and seated
In achromatic and expectant curves
Of buzzing, sunbeam-flecked, and overheated
Accommodation. Skins perspire ... But hark! ...
Begins the great *B minor Mass* of Bach.

The choir sings *Gloria in excelsis Deo*
With confident and well-conducted *brio*.
Outside, a motor-bike makes impious clatter,
Impinging on our Eighteenth-Century trammels.
God's periwigged: He takes a pinch of snuff.
The music's half-rococo. ... Does it matter
While those intense musicians shout the stuff
In Catholic Latin to the cultured mammals
Who agitate the pages of their scores? ...

Meanwhile, in Oxford sunshine out of doors,
Birds in collegiate gardens rhapsodize
Antediluvian airs of worm-thanksgiving.
To them the austere and buried Bach replies
With song that from ecclesiasmus cries
External *Resurrexit* to the living.

Hosanna in excelsis chants the choir
In pious contrapuntal jubilee.

47

Hosanna shrill the birds in sunset fire.
And Benedictus sings my heart to Me.

Early Chronology

Slowly the daylight left our listening faces.

Professor Brown with level baritone
Discoursed into the dusk.
                              Five thousand years
He guided us through scientific spaces
Of excavated History; till his lone
Roads of research grew blurred; and in our ears
Time was the rumoured tongues of vanished races,
And Thought a chartless Age of Ice and Stone.

The story ended: and the darkened air
Flowered while he lit his pipe; an aureole glowed
Enwreathed with smoke: the moment's match-light showed
His rosy face, broad brow, and smooth grey hair,
Backed by the crowded book-shelves.
                                     In his wake
An archæologist began to make
Assumptions about aqueducts (he quoted
Professor Sandstorm's book); and soon they floated
Through desiccated forests; mangled myths;
And argued easily round megaliths.

Beyond the college garden something glinted;
A copper moon climbed clear above black trees.
Some Lydian coin? . . . Professor Brown agrees
That copper coins *were* in that Culture minted.
But, as her whitening way aloft she took,
I thought she had a pre-dynastic look.

The Facts

Can a man face the facts of life and laugh? . . .
Swift faced them and died mad, deaf and diseased.
Shakespeare spoke out, went home, and wrote no more.
Oblivion was the only epitaph
They asked, as private persons, having eased
Their spirits of the burden that they bore.

The facts of life are fierce. One feels a wraith
When facing them with luminous lyric faith.
Daring to look within us, we discern
The jungle. To the jungle we return
More easily that most of us admit.
In this thought-riddled twentieth-century day
I cannot read — say 'Gulliver' — and feel gay,
Or share — in 'Lear' — the pleasure of the Pit.

1932.

Song, be my soul; set forth the fairest part
Of all that moved harmonious through my heart;
And gather me to your arms; for we must go
To childhood's garden when the moon is low
And over the leaf-shadow-latticed grass
The whispering wraiths of my dead selves repass.

Soul, be my song; return arrayed in white;
Lead home the loves that I have wronged and slain:
Bring back the summer dawns that banished night
With distant-warbling bird-notes after rain. . . .
Time's way-worn traveller I. And you, O song,
O soul, my Paradise laid waste so long.

Sing bravely in my heart, you patient birds
Who all this weary winter wait for spring;
Sing, till such wonder wakens in my words
As I have known long since, beyond all voicing, —
Strong with the beat of blood, wild on the wing,
Rebellious and rejoicing.

Watch with me, inward solemn influence,
Invisible, intangible, unkenned;
Wind of the darkness that shall bear me hence;
O life within my life, flame within flame,
Who mak'st me one with song that has no end,
And with that stillness whence my spirit came.

As I was walking in the gardens where
Spring touched the glooms with green, stole over me
A sense of wakening leaves that filled the air
With boding of Elysian days to be.

Cold was the music of the birds; and cold
The sunlight, shadowless with misty gold:
It seemed I stood with Youth on the calm verge
Of some annunciation that should bring
With flocks of silver angels, ultimate Spring
Whence all that life had longed for might emerge.

What you are I cannot say;
Only this I know full well —
When I touched your face to-day
Drifts of blossom flushed and fell.

Whence you came I cannot tell;
Only — with your joy you start
Chime on chime from bell on bell
In the cloisters of my heart.

While I seek you, far away,
(Yesterday, yesterday,)
Wakeful since we laughed and parted,
How can I recover
Joy that made Elysian-hearted,
Loved and lover?

Can my night-long thoughts regain
Time-locked loveliness and laughter?
Can your presence in my brain
Be rebuilt such æons after?
Can it be so far away —
Yesterday, yesterday?

Now when we two have been apart so long
And you draw near, I make you mine in song.
Waiting you in my thought's high lonely tower
That looks on starlit hushed Elysian gloom,
I know your advent certain as the flower
Of daybreak that on breathless vales shall bloom.

Oh, never hasten now; for time's all sweet,
And you are clad in the garment of my dreams:
Led by my heart's enchanted cry, your feet
Move with the murmur of forest-wandering streams

Through earth's adoring darkness to discover
The Paradise of your imperfect lover.

In me, past, present, future meet
To hold long chiding conference.
My lusts usurp the present tense
And strangle Reason in his seat.
My loves leap through the future's fence
To dance with dream-enfranchised feet.

In me the cave-man clasps the seer,
And garlanded Apollo goes
Chanting to Abraham's deaf ear.
In me the tiger sniffs the rose.
    Look in my heart, kind friends, and tremble,
    Since there your elements assemble.

Since thought is life, God's martyrdoms were good,
And saints are trumps, no matter what they did.
Therefore I celebrate Sebastian's blood,
And glory with Lorenzo on his grid,
And likewise with all victims, bruised by boulders,
Stabbed by sadistic swords, on pikes impaled,
Who propped their Paradise on bleeding shoulders
And bred tumultuous pomps when princes failed.

Thus for their murdered Master, — thus for his dreamed
Utopia, — from a crookèd Roman cross,
Heavenward on crimson clouds their conquest streamed
To touch His lips in life-redeeming loss.

What is Stonehenge? It is the roofless past;
Man's ruinous myth; his uninterred adoring
Of the unknown in sunrise cold and red;
His quest of stars that arch his doomed exploring.

And what is Time but shadows that were cast
By these storm-sculptured stones while centuries fled?

The stones remain; their stillness can outlast
The skies of history hurrying overhead.

Farewell to a Room

Room, while I stand outside you in the gloom,
Your tranquil-toned interior, void of me,
Seems part of my own self which I can see. . . .

Light, while I stand outside you in the night,
Shutting the door on what has housed so much,
Nor hand, nor eye, nor intellect could touch, —
Cell, to whose firelit walls I say farewell,
Could I condense five winters in one thought,
Then might I know my unknown self and tell
What our confederate silences have wrought.

'When I'm alone' — the words tripped off his tongue
As though to be alone were nothing strange.
'When I was young,' he said; 'when I was young. . . .'

I thought of age, and loneliness, and change.
I thought how strange we grow when we're alone,
And how unlike the selves that meet, and talk,
And blow the candles out, and say good-night.
Alone . . . The word is life endured and known.

It is the stillness where our spirits walk
And all but inmost faith is overthrown.

In the stars we have seen the strangeness of our state;
Wisdomless men, we have lifted up our eyes:
From the stars we have asked an augury of our fate,
And our speech has made them symbols of the wise.

O star that youth's awakening eyes have seen,
Sustain us in our nearness to the night:
And you, O storm-hid Hesperus, make serene
Our loss of this loved heritage of light.

Strangeness of Heart

When I have lost the power to feel the pang
Which first I felt in childhood when I woke
And heard the unheeding garden bird who sang
Strangeness of heart for me while morning broke;
Or when in latening twilight sure with spring,
Pausing on homeward paths along the wood,
No sadness thrills my thought while thrushes sing,
And I'm no more the listening child who stood
So many sunsets past and could not say
What wandering voices called from far away:
    When I have lost those simple spells that stirred
    My being with an untranslated song,
    Let me go home for ever; I shall have heard
    Death; I shall know that I have lived too long.

When Selfhood can discern no comfort for its cares,
Whither may I turn but to you whose strength my spirit shares?
   Where may I find but in you,
   Beethoven, Bach, Mozart,
   Timeless, eternally true,
   Heavens that may hold my heart?
   Rivers of peace that run beyond the setting sun,
   And where all names are one, green Paradise apart.

Grandeur of Ghosts

When I have heard small talk about great men
I climb to bed; light my two candles; then
Consider what was said; and put aside
What Such-a-one remarked and Someone-else replied.

They have spoken lightly of my deathless friends,
(Lamps for my gloom, hands guiding where I stumble,)
Quoting, for shallow conversational ends,
What Shelley shrilled, what Blake once wildly muttered. . . .

How can they use such names and be not humble?
I have sat silent; angry at what they uttered.
The dead bequeathed them life; the dead have said
What these can only memorize and mumble.

Alone, I hear the wind about my walls . . .
Wind of the city night, south-west and warm, —
Rain-burdened wind, your homely sound recalls
Youth; and a distant country-side takes form,

Comforting with memory-sight my town-taxed brain . . .
Wind from familiar fields and star-tossed trees,
You send me walking lonely through dark and rain
Before I'd lost my earliest ecstasies.

Wind of the city-lamps, you speak of home
And how into this homelessness I've come
Where all's uncertain but my will for power
To ask of life no more than life can earn . . .
Wind from the past, you bring me the last flower
From gardens where I'll nevermore return.

To an Eighteenth Century Poet

Old friend (for such you have lately grown to be
Since your tranquillities have tuned with mine),
Sitting alone, your poems on my knee,
In hours of contemplative candleshine,
I sometimes think your ghost revisits me
And lives upon my lips from line to line.

Dead though you are, the quiet-toned persistence
Of what you tell me with your sober skill
Reminds me how terrestrial existence
Plays tricks with death, and, unextinguished still,
Turns home in loveliest hauntings from the distance
Of antiquated years and works its will.

This is the power, the privilege, the pride
And rich morality of those who write
That hearts may be their highway. They shall ride
Conquering uncharted countries with the bright
Rewards of what they wrought in living light . . .
Who then shall dare to say that they have died?

To an Old Lady Dead

Old lady, when last year I sipped your tea
And wooed you with my deference to discuss
The elegance of your embroidery,
I felt no forethought of our meeting thus.
    Last week your age was 'almost eighty-three.'
    To-day you own the eternal over-plus.
    These moments are 'experience' for me;
    But not for you; not for a mutal 'us'.

I visit you unwelcomed; you've no time
Left to employ in afternoon politeness.
You've only Heaven's great stairway now to climb,
And your long load of years has changed to lightness.
    When Oxford belfries chime you do not hear,
    Nor in this mellow-toned autumnal brightness
    Observe an English-School-like atmosphere.
    You have inherited everlasting whiteness.

You lived your life in grove and garden shady
Of social Academe, good talk and taste:
But now you are a very quiet old lady,
Stiff, sacrosanct, and alabaster-faced.
    And, while I tip-toe awe-struck from your room,
    I fail to synthesize your earth-success
    With this, your semblance to a sculptured tomb
    That clasps a rosary of nothingness.

On Passing the New Menin Gate

Who will remember, passing through this Gate,
The unheroic Dead who fed the guns?
Who shall absolve the foulness of their fate, —
Those doomed, conscripted, unvictorious ones?
    Crudely renewed, the Salient holds its own.
    Paid are its dim defenders by this pomp;

Paid, with a pile of peace-complacent stone,
The armies who endured that sullen swamp.

Here was the world's worst wound. And here with pride
'Their name liveth for ever,' the Gateway claims.
Was ever an immolation so belied
As these intolerably nameless names?
Well might the Dead who struggled in the slime
Rise and deride this sepulchre of crime.

At the Grave of Henry Vaughan

Above the voiceful windings of a river
An old green slab of simply graven stone
Shuns notice, overshadowed by a yew.
Here Vaughan lies dead, whose name flows on for ever
Through pastures of the spirit washed with dew
And starlit with eternities unknown.

Here sleeps the Silurist; the loved physician;
The face that left no portraiture behind;
The skull that housed white angels and had vision
Of daybreak through the gateways of the mind.
    Here faith and mercy, wisdom and humility
    (Whose influence shall prevail for evermore)
    Shine. And this lowly grave tells Heaven's tranquillity.
    And here stand I, a suppliant at the door.

A Midnight Interior

To-night while I was pondering in my chair
I saw for the first time a circle of brightness
Made by my patient lamp up on the ceiling.
It shone like a strange flower; and then my stare
Discovered an arctic snowstorm in that whiteness;
And then some pastoral vale of rayed revealing.

White flowers were in a bowl beside my book;
In midnight's miracle of light they glowed,
And every petal there in silence showed
My life the way to wonder with a look.

O inwardness of trust, — intelligence, —
Release my soul through every door of sense:
Give me new sight; O grant me strength to find
From lamp and flower simplicity of mind.

One Who Watches

We are all near to death. But in my friends
I am forewarned too closely of that nearness.
Death haunts their days that are; in him descends
The darkness that shall change their living dearness
  To something different, made within my mind
  By memories and recordings and convenings
  Of voices heard through veils and faces blind
  To the kind light of my autumnal gleanings.

Not so much for myself I feel that fear
As for all those in whom my loves must die;
Thus, like some hooded death, I stand apart
And in their happiest moments I can hear
Silence unending, when those lives must lie
Hoarded like happy summers in my heart.

I cannot pray with my head,
Nor aspire from bended knees;
But I saw in a dream the dead
Moving among green trees.

59

I saw the living green
Uprising from the rock.
This have I surely seen,
Though the morning mind may mock.

All-Souls' Day

Close-wrapped in living thought I stand
Where death and daybreak divide the land, —
Death and daybreak on either hand
For exit and for entry;
While shapes like wind-blown shadows pass,
Lost and lamenting, 'Alas, alas,
This body is only shrivelling grass,
And the soul a starlit sentry
Who guards, and as he comes and goes,
Points now to daybreak's burning rose,
And now toward worldhood's charnel close
Leans with regretless warning' . . .

I hear them thus — O thus I hear
My doomed companions crowding near,
Until my faith, absolved from fear,
Sings out into the morning,
And tells them how we travel far,
From life to life, from star to star;
Exult, unknowing what we are;
And quell the obscene derision
Of demon-haunters in our heart
Who work for worms and have no part
In Thee, O ultimate power, who art
Our victory and our vision.

The Power and the Glory

Let there be life, said God. And what He wrought
Went past in myriad marching lives, and brought

This hour, this quiet room, and my small thought
Holding invisible vastness in its hands.

Let there be God, say I. And what I've done
Goes onward like the splendour of the sun
And rises up in rapture and is one
With the white power of conscience that commands.

Let life be God. . . . What wail of fiend or wraith
Dare mock my glorious angel where he stands
To fill my dark with fire, my heart with faith?

The wisdom of the world is this. To say, *There is*
No other wisdom but to gulp what time can give.
    To guard no inward vision winged with mysteries;
    To hear no voices haunt the hurrying hours we live;
    To keep no faith with ghostly friends; never to know
    Vigils of sorrow crowned when loveless passions fade . . .
From wisdom such as this to find my gloom I go,
Companioned by those powers who keep me unafraid.

A flower has opened in my heart . . .
What flower is this, what flower of spring,
What simple, secret thing?
It is the peace that shines apart,
The peace of daybreak skies that bring
Clear song and wild swift wing.

Heart's miracle of inward light,
What powers unknown have sown your seed
And your perfection freed? . . .
O flower within me wondrous white,
I know you only as my need
And my unsealèd sight.

An Emblem

Poet, plant your tree
On the upward way;
Aromatic bay
Plant, that men may see
Beauty greenly growing
There in storm or shine,
And through boughs divine
Freedom bravely blowing.

Vigils

Lone heart, learning
By one light burning,
Slow discerning of worldhood's worth;
Soul, awaking
By night and taking
Roads forsaking enchanted earth:
Man, unguided
And self-divided,
Clocked by silence which tells decay;
You that keep
In a land asleep
One light burning till break of day:
You whose vigil
Is deed and sigil,
Bond and service of lives afar, —
Seek, in seeing

62

Your own blind being,
Peace, remote in the morning star.

December Stillness

December stillness, teach me through your trees
That loom along the west, one with the land,
The veiled evangel of your mysteries.
   While nightfall, sad and spacious, on the down
   Deepens, and dusk imbues me, where I stand,
   With grave diminishings of green and brown,
   Speak, roofless Nature, your instinctive words;
   And let me learn your secret from the sky,
   Following a flock of steadfast-journeying birds
   In lone remote migration beating by.
December stillness, crossed by twilight roads,
Teach me to travel far and bear my loads.

It was the love of life, when I was young,
Which led me out in summer to explore
The daybreak world. A bird's first notes were sung
For childhood standing at the garden door.
That loneliness it was which made me wise
When I looked out and saw
Dark trees against the strangely brightening skies
And learnt the love of earth that is my law.

The love of life is my religion still.
Steadfast through rigorous nights, companioned only
By what I am and what I strive to be, —
I seek no mystery now beyond the hill
And wait no change but to become more lonely,
No freedom till the sleep that sets me free.

My past has gone to bed. Upstairs in clockless rooms
My past is fast asleep. But mindsight reillumes
Here in my ruminant head the days where dust lies deep.

Sleep-walkers empty-eyed come strangely down the stairs.
These are my selves, — once proud, once passionate with young
     prayers,
Once vehement with vows. I know not when they died,
Those ignorant selves. . . . Meanwhile my self sits brooding here
In the house where I was born. Dwindling, they disappear.
Me they did not foresee. But in their looks I find
Simplicities unlearned long since and left behind.

In Sicily

Because we two can never again come back
On life's one forward track, —
Never again first-happily explore
This valley of rocks and vines and orange-trees,
Half Biblical and half Hesperides,
With dark blue seas calling from a shell-strewn shore:
    By the strange power of Spring's resistless green,
    Let us be true to what we have shared and seen,
    And as our amulet this idyll save.
    And since the unreturning day must die,
    Let it for ever be lit by an evening sky
    And the wild myrtle grow upon its grave.

Revisitation

(W.H.R.R.)

What voice revisits me this night? What face
To my heart's room returns?
From that perpetual silence where the grace
Of human sainthood burns

Hastes he once more to harmonize and heal?
I know not. Only I feel
His influence undiminished.
And his life's work, in me and many, unfinished.

O fathering friend and scientist of good,
Who in solitude, one bygone summer's day,
And in throes of bodily anguish, passed away
From dream and conflict and research-lit lands
Of ethnologic learning, — even as you stood
Selfless and ardent, resolute and gay,
So in this hour, in strange survival stands
Your ghost, whom I am powerless to repay.

The Merciful Knight

Swift, in a moment's thought, our lastingness is wrought
From life, the transient wing.
Swift, in a moment's light, he mercy found, that knight
Who rode alone in spring . . .
The knight who sleeps in stone with ivy overgrown
Knew this miraculous thing.
In a moment of the years the sun, like love through tears,
Shone where the rain went by.
In a world where armoured men made swords their strength and
    then
Rode darkly out to die,
One heart was there estranged ; one heart, one heart was changed
While the cloud crossed the sun . . .
Mercy from long ago, be mine that I may know
Life's lastingness begun.

Eulogy of My House

House, though you've harboured grave-yards-full of lives
Since on your first foundations walls were built,

In your essential atmosphere survives
No sense of men's malignity and guilt.
Bad times you must have known, and human wrongness;
Yet your plain wisdom leaves it all behind you,
Within whose walls tranquillity and strongness
Keep watch on life. Dependable I find you.

Much good has been your making. I can feel
That when your ghosts revisit you they steal
From room to room like moonlight long ago:
And if some voice from silence haunts my head
I only wonder who it was that said —
'House, I am here because I loved you so.'

In Heytesbury Wood

Not less nor more than five and forty years ago
The old lord went along the ornamental ride;
For the last time he walked there, tired and very slow;
Saw the laburnum's golden chains, the glooming green
Of bowery box-trees; stood and looked farewell, and sighed
For roots that held his heart and summers that he'd seen.

And then, maybe, he came again there, year by year,
To watch, as dead men do, and see — who knows how clear? —
That vista'd paradise which in his time had thriven;
Those trees to which in cogitating strolls he'd given
Perennial forethought, — branches that he'd lopped and
        cherished:
Came, and saw sad neglect; dense nettles; favourites felled
Or fallen in gales and left to rot; came and beheld
How with succeeding seasons his laburnums perished.

'Return', I think, 'next summer, and you'll find such change, —
Walking, some low-lit evening, in the whispering wood, —
As will refresh your eyes and do them ghostly good;
See redolence befriend, neglect no more estrange;

See plumed acacia and the nobly tranquil bay;
Laburnums too, now small as in the prosperous prime
Of your well-ordered distant mid-Victorian time . . .'
Thus I evoke him; thus he looks and goes his way
Along that path we call the ornamental ride —
The old slow lord, the ghost whose trees were once his pride.

A Local Train of Thought

Alone, in silence, at a certain time of night,
Listening, and looking up from what I'm trying to write,
I hear a local train along the Valley. And 'There
Goes the one-fifty', think I to myself; aware
That somehow its habitual travelling comforts me,
Making my world seem safer, homelier, sure to be
The same to-morrow; and the same, one hopes, next year.
'There's peacetime in that train.' One hears it disappear
With needless warning whistle and rail-resounding wheels.
'That train's quite like an old familiar friend', one feels.

'A View of Old Exeter'

Pyne, a small honest painter, well content
To limn our English landscapes, worked and went,
From 1800 onward, seventy years,
Then left the world to louden in men's ears.
Here's his 'Old Exeter'; much eyed by me
Since (how time flits!) full fifteen years ago
I bought it cheap and carried it home to be
A window on my wall making me know
Old Exeter, affectionately recorded
In the now slow paced 'fifties.
                              Glancing down
From some neglected meadow near the town,
He hummed and sketched that I might be afforded
This purview of the past's provincial peace.

For J. B. Pyne Old Exeter was good;
Cows in his foreground grazed and strolled and stood:
For J. B. Pyne Victorian clumps of trees
Were golden in a bland October breeze:
Large clouds, like safe investments, loitered by;
And distant Dartmoor loomed in sombre blue.
Perpetuator of that shifting sky,
It never crossed his mind that he might do
From death such things as make me stare and sigh, —
Sigh for that afternoon he thus depicted, —
That simpler world from which we've been evicted.

Here his prim figures cruise and sit and drive
In crinolines as when they were alive.
Out of the town that man and wife are going
In smart new gig, complacently unknowing
Of their great-grandchild's air-raid-worried mind:
Into the town those gentlewomen are walking
Attuned to life, of the new Bishop talking —
Pleased that the eighteenth century's left behind,
And civically unconscious, I conjecture,
Of what it gave them in good architecture.
That group beside the cypresses adds calm
And absent-minded momentary charm
To the industrious artist's composition . . .
When J. B. Pyne's, this was a Devon Day.
For me it shines far far — too far — away;
For time has changed this 'View' into a Vision.

Metamorphosis

Sandys sat translating Ovid. Both his hands
Were busy. Busy was his curious mind.
Each note he wrote was news from fabled lands.
He hob-nobbed with Pythagoras, calm and kind.
In a quaint narrow age, remote from this,
Sat Sandys translating *Metamorphosis*.

The scholarship is obsolete, and the verse
Pedestrian perhaps. Yet, while I turn
His friendly folio pages (none the worse
For emblematic worm-holes) I discern
Not Nature preying on itself, but Time
Revealed by rich humanity in rhyme.

Two Old Ladies

Here's an old lady, almost ninety-one.
Fragile in dark blue velvet, from her chair
She talks to me about Lord Palmerston,
With whom her father 'often took the air'.
I watch her tiny black-lace-mittened hands —
When tea-time's ended — slowly crumble a rusk
For feeding peacocks with. Reflective stands
My memory-mirror in the autumn dusk.

Memory records the scene; and straightway plays
One of its dream-like unexpected tricks;
Transports me forty years to summer days
On time's first page, when I was only six . . .
Miss Clara, deaf and old, alert and queer,
With scraps of bread heaped on a dark blue dish,
Conducts me — I can catch her voice quite clear —
Out to the lily-pond to feed the fish.

Blunden's Beech

I named it Blunden's Beech; and no one knew
That this — of local beeches — was the best.
Remembering lines by Clare, I'd sometimes rest
Contentful on the cushioned moss that grew
Between its roots. Finches, a flitting crew,
Chirped their concerns. Wiltshire, from east to west,

Contained my tree. And Edmund never guessed
How he was there with me till dusk and dew.

Thus, fancy-free from ownership and claim,
The mind can make its legends live and sing
And grow to be the genius of some place.
And thus, where sylvan shadows held a name,
The thought of Poetry will dwell, and bring
To summer's idyll an unheeded grace.

Wealth of Awareness

Stars burning bright in summer night; and I
Standing alone with lifetime on this lawn;
Smelling the dew that soaks the sunburnt grass,
Alone with moth-winged gloom and folded flowers
And secret stirrings, hours away from dawn.

One with these garden silences that pass,
I know that life is in my saturate sense
Of growth and memories of what lifetime meant.
I am yet young with my unheard unspent
Awareness of slow-stored intransience:
And still, where trees like sentinels look for day,
I feel what all have felt and know what none can say.

Meeting and Parting

My self reborn, I look into your eyes;
While you, unknowing, look your first time on me.
Thus will *you* stand when life within me dies,
And you, full knowing, my parting presence see.

Alone I stand before my new-born son;
Alone he lies before me, doomed to live.

Beloved, when I am dying and all is done,
Look on my face and say that you forgive.

To My Son

Go, and be gay;
You are born into the dazzling light of day.
Go, and be wise;
You are born upon an earth which needs new eyes.
Go, and be strong;
You are born into a world where love rights wrong.
Go, and be brave;
Possess your soul; that you alone can save.

The Child at the Window

Remember this, when childhood's far away;
The sunlight of a showery first spring day;
You from your house-top window laughing down,
And I, returned with whip-cracks from a ride,
On the great lawn below you, playing the clown.
Time blots our gladness out. Let this with love abide . . .

The brave March day; and you, not four years old,
Up in your nursery world — all heaven for me.
Remember this — the happiness I hold —
In far off springs I shall not live to see;
The world one map of wastening war unrolled,
And you, unconscious of it, setting my spirit free.

For you must learn, beyond bewildering years,
How little things beloved and held are best.
The windows of the world are blurred with tears,
And troubles come like cloud-banks from the west.
Remember this, some afternoon in spring,
When your own child looks down and makes your sad heart sing.

71

Progressions

A lovely child alone, singing to himself serenely, —
Playing with pebbles in an unfrequented garden
Through drowse of summer afternoon where time drifts greenly.

A youth, impassioned by he knows not what, exploring
Delusive labyrinths in errors age will pardon, —
A youth, all ignorance, all grace, his dreams adoring.

A man, confounded by the facts of life that bind him
Prometheus-like to rocks where vulture doubts assail him, —
A man, with blank discarded youthfulness behind him.

A mind, matured in wearying bones, returning slowly
Toward years revisioned richly while fruitions fail him, —
A mind, renouncing hopes and finding lost loves holy.

Old Music

Like the notes of an old violin,
Thoughts talk to me within
My mind, that shuttered room.
Like luminous portraits, hung
On walls where I once was young,
Dead friends pervade the gloom.

Decades of mellowing went
To make this calmed content,
This mental vintagement
Of youth's harsh tasting wine . . .
Old violin, play on
Till heart-held thought be gone:
Old friends whose charity shone
For me, be memory-mine.

Silent Service

Now, multifold, let Britain's patient power
Be proven within us for the world to see.
None are exempt from service in this hour;
And vanquished in ourselves we dare not be.
　　Now, for a sunlit future, we can show
　　The clenched resolved endurance that defies
　　Daemons in dark, — and toward that future go
　　With earth's defended freedom in our eyes.
　　In every separate soul let courage shine —
　　A kneeling angel holding faith's front-line.

May 23, 1940.

Release

One winter's end I much bemused my head
In tasked attempts to drive it up to date
With what the undelighting moderns said
　　Forecasting human fate.

And then, with nothing unforeseen to say
And no belief or unbelief to bring,
Came, in its old unintellectual way,
　　The first real day of spring.

Euphrasy

The large untidy February skies —
Some cheerful starlings screeling on a tree —
West wind and low-shot sunlight in my eyes —
　　Is this decline for me?

The feel of winter finishing once more —
Sense of the present as a tale half told —

The land of life to look at and explore —
Is this, then, to grow old?

At Max Gate

Old Mr. Hardy, upright in his chair,
Courteous to visiting acquaintance chatted
With unaloof alertness while he patted
The sheep dog whose society he preferred.
He wore an air of never having heard
That there was much that needed putting right.
Hardy, the Wessex wizard, wasn't there.
Good care was taken to keep him out of sight.

Head propped on hand, he sat with me alone,
Silent, the log fire flickering on his face.
Here was the seer whose words the world had known.
Someone had taken Mr. Hardy's place.

To My Mother

I watch you on your constant way,
In selfless duty long grown grey;
And to myself I say
That I have lived my life to learn
How lives like your unasking earn
Aureoles that guide, and burn
    In heart's remembrance when the proud
    Who snared the suffrage of the crowd
    Are dumb and dusty browed . . .
For you live onward in my thought
Because you have not sought
Rewards that can be bought.
And so when I remember you
I think of all things rich and true
That I have reaped and wrought.

74

Redemption

I thought; These multitudes we hold in mind —
This host of souls redeemed —
Out of the abysm of the ages came —
Out of the spirit of man — devised or dreamed.

I thought; To the Invisible I am blind;
No angels tread my nights with feet of flame;
No mystery is mine —
No whisper from that world beyond my sense.

I think; If through some chink in me could shine
But once — O but one ray
From that all-hallowing and eternal day,
Asking no more of Heaven I would go hence.

A Prayer to Time

Time, that anticipates eternities
And has an art to resurrect the rose;
Time, whose lost siren song at evening blows
With sun-flushed cloud shoreward on topping seas;
Time, arched by planets lonely in the vast
Sadness that darkens with the fall of day;
Time, unexplored elysium; and the grey
Death-shadow'd pyramid that we name the past —
    Magnanimous Time, patient with man's vain glory;
    Ambition's road; Lethe's awaited guest;
    Time, hearkener to the stumbling passionate story
    Of human failure humanly confessed;
    Time, on whose stair we dream our hopes of heaven,
    Help us to judge ourselves, and so be shriven.

Ultimate Values

The hour grows late, and I outlive my friends,
Remaining, since I must, with memoried mind
That for consolement deepeningly depends
On hoarded time, enriched and redesigned.
So is it with us all. And thus we find
Endeared survivals that our thought defends.

What now, from eyed experience, haunts my ears,
Endenizened within me, heart and head?
Mostly those things which touched the source of tears,
Those word-illumined moments, seen and said,
Those wisdoms, mortalised beyond the years
By simplest human utterance of the dead.

On Scratchbury Camp

Along the grave green downs, this idle afternoon,
Shadows of loitering silver clouds, becalmed in blue,
Bring, like unfoldment of a flower, the best of June.

Shadows outspread in spacious movement, always you
Have dappled the downs and valleys at this time of year,
While larks, ascending shrill, praised freedom as they flew.
Now, through that song, a fighter-squadron's drone I hear
From Scratchbury Camp, whose turfed and cowslip'd rampart
    seems
More hill than history, ageless and oblivion-blurred.

I walk the fosse, once manned by bronze and flint-head spear;
On war's imperious wing the shafted sun-ray gleams:
One with the warm sweet air of summer stoops the bird.

Cloud shadows, drifting slow like heedless daylight dreams,
Dwell and dissolve; uncircumstanced they pause and pass.
I watch them go. My horse, contented, crops the grass.

A Fallodon Memory

One afternoon I watched him as he stood
In the twilight of his wood.
Among the firs he'd planted, forty years away,
Tall, and quite still, and almost blind,
World patience in his face, stood Edward Grey;
Not listening,
For it was at the end of summer, when no birds sing:
Only the bough's faint dirge accompanied his mind
Absorbed in some Wordsworthian slow self-communing.

In lichen-coloured homespun clothes he seemed
So merged with stem and branch and twinkling leaves
That almost I expected, looking away, to find
When glancing there again, that I had daylight dreamed
His figure, as when some trick of sun and shadow deceives.

But there he was, haunting heart-known ancestral ground;
Near to all Nature; and in that nearness somehow strange;
Whose native humour, human-simple yet profound,
And strength of spirit no calamity could change.
To whom, designed for countrified contentments, came
Honours unsought and unrewarding foreign fame:
And, at the last, that darkened world wherein he moved
In memoried deprivation of life once learnt and loved.

A Proprietor

A meditative man
Walks in this wood, and calls each tree his own:
Yet the green track he treads is older than
Recorded English history:
His feet, while moving on towards times unknown,
Travel from traceless mystery.
Wondering what manner of men
Will walk there in the problem'd future when

Those trees he planted are long fallen or felled,
He twirls a white wild violet in his fingers
As others may when he's no more beheld,
Nor memory of him lingers.

Cleaning the Candelabrum

While cleaning my old six-branched candelabrum
(Which disconnects in four and twenty parts)
I think how other hands its brass have brightened,
And wonder what was happening in their hearts:
I wonder what they mused about — those ghosts —
In what habitual prosy-morning'd places,
Who furbished these reflections, humming softly
With unperplexed or trouble-trodden faces.

While rubbing up the ring by which one lifts it,
I visualise some Queen Anne country squire
Guiding a guest from dining-room to parlour
Where port and filberts wait them by the fire:
Or — in the later cosmos of Miss Austen —
Two spinsters, wavering shadows on a wall,
Conferring volubly about Napoleon
And what was worn at the Assembly Ball.

Then, thought-reverting to the man who made it
With long-apprenticed unpresuming skill,
When earth was yet unwarned of Electricity
And rush-lights gave essential service still,
I meditate upon mankind's advancement
From flint sparks into million-volted glare
That shows us everything except the future —
And leaves us not much wiser than we were.

Dim lights have had their day; wax candles even
Produce a conscious 'period atmosphere'.

78

But brass out-twinkles time; my candelabrum
Persists well on towards its three hundredth year,
And has illuminated, one might say,
Much vista'd history, many vanished lives . . .
Meanwhile for me, outside my open window,
The twilight blackbird flutes, and spring arrives.

Associates

It was not thus while we were young —
Not thus for us
When breath was bold and heart hope toward
The future flung,
And hours could shine like towers where bells
Are wildly rung.

It was not so for you and me —
Not so, we know,
When body and being owned the earth
And each was free.
A way-worn man within you dwells,
And I am he.

The Tasking

To find rewards of mind with inward ear
Through silent hours of seeking;
To put world sounds behind and hope to hear
Instructed spirit speaking:

Sometimes to catch a clue from selfhood's essence
And ever that revealment to be asking;
This — and through darkness to divine God's presence—
I take to be my tasking.

Another Spring

Aged self, disposed to lose his hold on life,
Looks down, at winter's ending, and perceives
Continuance in some crinkled primrose leaves.
A noise of nesting rooks in tangled trees.
Stillness — inbreathed, expectant. Shadows that bring
Cloud-castled thoughts from downland distances.
Eyes, ears are old. But not the sense of spring.

Look, listen, live, some inward watcher warns.
*Absorb this moment's meaning: and be wise
With hearts whom the first primrose purifies.*

An Epitome

Just thinking . . . Yet it may be that
My thought, which for a moment held
What seemed mind-life's epitome
From infanthood to eld,
Spoke the one word in all my time
To make endured existence known
Even as it is. *Accept your soul.
Be evermore alone.*

Renewals

I said to downcast eyes —
Look up; accept surprise
Which waits, all welcomings.
I said to shuttered ears —
Heed how earth music nears
On wonder's wind-swept strings.

Unquesting heart I told
To be made manifold

Through love's resurgent will.
I said to fitful mind —
Put discontents behind;
Be silent and grow still.

The Humbled Heart

Go your seeking, soul.
Mine the proven path of time's foretelling.
Yours accordance with some mysteried whole.
I am but your passion-haunted dwelling.

Bring what news you can,
Stranger, loved of body's humbled heart.
Say one whispered word to mortal man
From that peace whereof he claims you part.

Hither-hence, my guest,
Blood and bone befriend, where you abide
Till withdrawn to share some timeless quest.
I am but the brain that dreamed and died.

A Chord

On stillness came a chord,
While I, the instrument,
Knew long-withheld reward:
Gradual the glory went;
Vibrating, on and on,
Toward harmony unheard,
Till dark where sanctus shone;
Lost, once a living word.

But in me yet abode
The given grace though gone;

The love, the lifted load,
The answered orison.

Lenten Illuminations

I

Not properly Catholic, some might say, to like it best
When no one's in the cool white church that few frequent
These sober-skied vocational afternoons in Lent.
There's sanctity in stillness, let it be confessed,
For one addicted much to meditationment —
One who has found this church a place full of replies
Given to what, wordless in him, asked that heart be learned
À Kempis lessons; toward the invisible, new eyes
In more than meditational consciousness be turned.

This afternoon it seemed unconvert self came in,
Puzzled to perceive one at the altar rails, unminding;
Could this be he — hereafter offered him to win,
And faith revealed wheretoward he pilgrim'd without finding?

O unforeknowing Ego, visitant in thought,
How were you thus the captive of that banished being?
Was it ordained — the long delayed deliverance brought —
The mercy that made plain your path? . . . O unforeseeing
Sad self, let's be together, now fortunate in freeing.

II

What were you up to — going into churches all those years
Of faith unfaithful? . . . Kneeling respectfully when others knelt,
But never a moment while reflective there alone.
The aids were manifest; but only for your eyes and ears,
In anthems, organ music, shaft-aspiring stone,
And jewelled windows into which your mind might melt.
The sanctuary unseen was there; but not for you; not by the empty
        altar shown;

82

Not in the Crucifix. (Though each Good Friday you had felt
Almost unbearable the idea of how He died.)
From your default His face seemed ever turned aside.
Not then for you the arisen Word — not then the wrought
    remedial gift of tears.

How came it (ask your Angel — ask that vigilant voice)
That you this comfort found — that thus it grew to be —
This close, child-minded calm? . . . Look; those five candles lit
For five who have prayed your peace. (Candles were ever your
    choice
To tranquillize the mind, since boyhood.) They are what they are.
Two pennies for each. But Candlemas tells purity.
And we are told their innocent radiance will remit
Our errors. Although the lights of everlastingness, as someone said,
Can seem, for us poor souls, to dream so faint and far,
When at our broken orisons we kneel, unblest, unbenefited.

While you were in your purgatorial time, you used to say
That though Creation's God remained so lost, such aeons away,
Somehow He would reveal Himself to you — some day !
For Him, the Living God, your soul and flesh could only cry
    aloud.
In watches of the night, when world event with devildom went
    dark,
You implored illumination. But never being bowed
Obedient — never conceived an aureoled instance, an assuring
    spark.

Outcast and unprotected contours of the soul,
Why in those hallowed minsters could they find no home,
When nothing appeared more unpredictable than this — your
    whole
Influence, relief, resultancy received from Rome?
Look. Robed in white and blue, earth's best loved Lady stands;
Mother Immaculate; Name that shines to intercede.
Born on her birthday feast, until last year your hands
Kindled no candle, paid her heavenliness no heed.

Is it not well, that now you call yourself her child —
You and this rosary, at which — twelve months ago, — you might
   have shrugged and smiled?

This day twelve months ago — it was Ash Wednesday — one
Mid-way between us two toward urgent hope fulfilled
Strove with submission. Arduous — forbidding — then to meet
Inflexible Authority. While the work was willed,
The riven response from others to the task undone
Daunted a mind confused with ferment, incomplete:
There seemed so much renunciant consequence involved,
When independent questioning self should yield, indubitant and
   absolved.

III

This, then, brought our new making. Much emotional stress —
Call it conversion; but the word can't cover such good.
It was like being in love with ambient blessedness —
In love with life transformed — life breathed afresh, though yet half
   understood.
There had been many byways for the frustrate brain,
All leading to illusions lost and shrines forsaken . . .
One road before us now — one guidance for our gain —
One morning light — whatever the world's weather — wherein
   wide-eyed to waken.

IV

This is the time of year when, even for the old,
Youngness comes knocking on the heart with undefined
Aches and announcements — blurred felicities foretold,
And (obvious utterance) wearying winter left behind.

I never felt it more than now, when out beyond these safening walls
Sculptured with Stations of the Cross, spring-confident,
   unburdened, bold,
The first March blackbird overheard to forward vision flutes and
   calls.

84

You could have said this simple thing, old self, in any previous year.
But not to that one ritual flame — to that all-answering Heart
    abidant here.

Sight Sufficient

God, on the gloom divine wheretoward I pray,
You send no sign, no doubt-redeeming ray;
Nor manifest, for this unwisdom'd one,
The faith that blest his pilgrim path begun.

O purpose of my prayer, breath of my being,
Your inward light I share through sightless seeing;
Your love can but be told beyond blind thought
That knows your peace enfold believement brought.

Rogation

Wisdom remote from reason, mysteried Word,
Shrined for reverberant precincts of the soul,
Above blind-led belief be held and heard;
Need of the nescient, radiate and enrol.

Indwelt redemption, doubted and denied;
Concord no sanctity could comprehend;
Mercy immeasurable and multiplied;
World watcher, armed and influent to befriend;
Hope of humility, resistless rood,
Beyond our bodements bring beatitude.

Arbor Vitae

For grace in me divined
This metaphor I find:

A tree.
　　How can that be?

This tree all winter through
Found no green work to do —
No life
　　Therein ran rife.

But with an awoken year
What surge of sap is here —
What flood
　　In branch and bud.

So grace in me can hide —
Be darkened and denied —
Then once again
　　Vesture my every vein.

Unfoldment

Tight buds of daffodil
Plucked where the wind blew chill
　　In Lent begun,
Blessed by this well-warmed room
Unsheathe themselves, for whom
　　The lamp's their sun.

So, when to prayer I turn
And my dark being discern
　　Life-locked from Thee,
Unfold it as a flower,
That I may know Thy power
　　Befriending me.

A Prayer at Pentecost

Master musician, I have overheard you,
Labouring in litanies of heart to word you.
Be noteless now. Our duologue is done.

Spirit, who speak'st by silences, remake me;
To light of unresistant faith awake me,
That with resolvèd requiem I be one.

Awaitment

Eternal, to this momentary thing —
This mind — Thy sanctuary of stillness bring.
Within that unredeemed aliveness, live:
And through Thy sorrowless sacrament forgive.
  Let me be lost; and lose myself in Thee.
  Let me be found; and find my soul set free.

Proven Purpose

Because I have believed, I bid my mind be still.
Therein is now conceived Thy hid yet sovereign Will.
Because I set all thought aside in seeking Thee,
Thy proven purpose wrought abideth blest in me.
Because I can no more exist but in Thy being,
Blindly these eyes adore; sightless are taught new seeing.

A Prayer in Old Age

Bring no expectance of a heaven unearned
No hunger for beatitude to be
Until the lesson of my life is learned
Through what Thou didst for me.

Bring no assurance of redeemèd rest
No intimation of awarded grace
Only contrition, cleavingly confessed
To Thy forgiving face.

I ask one world of everlasting loss
In all I am, that other world to win.
My nothingness must kneel below Thy Cross.
There let new life begin.

Index of First Lines

90

Lone heart, learning, 62
Lost in the swamp and welter of the pit, 33

Master musician, I have overheard you, 87
Music of whispering trees, 20
My music-loving Self this afternoon, 47
My past has gone to bed. Upstairs in clockless rooms, 64
My self reborn, I look into your eyes; 70

No doubt they'll soon get well; the shock and strain, 32
Not less nor more than five and forty years ago, 66
Not properly Catholic, some might say, to like it best, 82
Now, multifold, let Britain's patient power, 73
Now when we two have been apart so long, 51

October's bellowing anger breaks and cleaves, 32
'Of course you saw the Villa d'Este Gardens', 44
Old as a toothless Regius Professor, 46
Old friend (for such you have lately grown to be, 56
Old lady, when last year I sipped your tea, 57
Old Mr. Hardy, upright in his chair, 74
On stillness came a chord, 81
One afternoon I watched him as he stood, 77
One winter's end I much bemused my head, 73

Poet, plant your tree, 62
Propped on a stick he viewed the August weald; 19
Pyne, a small honest painter, well content, 67

Remember this, when childhood's far away; 71
Room, while I stand outside you in the gloom, 53

Sandys sat translating Ovid. Both his hands, 68
Shaken from sleep, and numbed and scarce awake, 29
Since thought is life, God's martyrdoms were good, 52
Sing bravely in my heart, you patient birds, 50
Sleep; and my song shall build about your bed, 39
Slowly the daylight left our listening faces, 48

91

When I was young my heart and head were light, 37
When I'm alone — the words tripped off his tongue, 53
When I'm among a blaze of lights, 14
When I'm asleep, dreaming and lulled and warm, — , 30
When Selfhood can discern no comfort for its cares, 55
When you are standing at your hero's grave, 35
While cleaning my old six-branched candelabrum, 78
While I seek you, far away, 51
Who will remember, passing through this Gate, 57
Why do you lie with your legs ungainly huddled, 35
Wisdom remote from reason, mysteried word, 85

You love us when we're heroes, home on leave, 28
You were glad to-night; and now you've gone away, 38
Your dextrous wit will haunt us long, 37